ESCAPE
VELOCITY!

Propel your organization past the gravity
of good into the space of greatness

Laird J Mott, mba, mcc, csfc

author HOUSE

AuthorHouse™
1663 Liberty Drive
Bloomington, IN 47403
www.authorhouse.com
Phone: 1 (800) 839-8640

This is a work of fiction. All of the characters, names, incidents, organizations, and dialogue in this novel are either the products of the author's imagination or are used fictitiously.

Published by AuthorHouse 11/13/2019

ISBN: 978-1-4969-1932-8 (sc)
ISBN: 978-1-4969-1933-5 (hc)
ISBN: 978-1-4969-1934-2 (e)

Library of Congress Control Number: 2019918170

Print information available on the last page.

This book is printed on acid-free paper.

My Appreciation To

I want to thank my good friend John Kreifels and business/life coach who actually had a case that was similar although I have fictionalized much of it so the story can be told.

Also, my business partner, Lynn Salathiel who demonstrates the best qualities of a business coach and helped me get through very tough times while writing this. She unlocked the writer's block and helped form many pages of material ideas and story line.

Contents

Chapter One

THIS ISN'T FUN ANYMORE

Mike was drifting in and out of sleep and as he rolled over for the hundredth time that night. His mind continued to repeat all possible scenarios about the coming workday. These sleepless nights had become the norm over the last several months. "When did work cease to be fun?" Mike thought. He mused, "If it wasn't for the employees it would be alright". He wondered how his dad did this every day for his whole life. Just then the alarm went off and his heart sank at the realization of another day at the grist mill.

Of course, it wasn't really a grist mill; it was an ambulance company in a large metropolitan city. His grandfather started the company, his father had run it, and now he was the company's president. He had taken over in his early thirties when his dad had a stroke. Mike had a primary teaching degree and had no confidence that he could handle the business when he took over. And now, after 13 years, that lack of confidence had turned to fear. Mike felt totally inadequate to run the company but, every day he put on his game face. The stress made him tired, frustrated and he longed for an opportunity to go back to teaching again.

As he was driving to the office, he wondered where he went wrong. He thought his numbers looked good, showing consistently between a 7 to 9% net income. He kept costs down by applying his grandfather's old saying, "fix it up, wear it out, make it do, or do without". His ambulances were proud examples of that kind of thinking and yeah, just about everything else too.

Sales didn't seem to be a problem, every year he would pick up new contracts to replace the customers who had left. However, his revenues had been level over the last three years and his business had not grown. Mike had justified this trend with the thought that his company and the industry were at the mature stage and there wasn't much more room for growth. However, the news he heard yesterday had really disturbed him. A friend who was a real estate agent had let him know that another ambulance company was looking for office space to expand their operations in his territory. Why would they do that if the market was saturated? Was he missing something?

As Mike pulled into his reserved parking space he saw Jeremy Perkins get out of his car and begin to walk towards him. Mike really wanted to avoid him. Jeremy was the union organizer who was working hard to organize the EMTs and drivers in his shop.

"Mr. Post", Jeremy called out, "wait up". Mike stopped and watched the overweight weasel in the red power tie huff his way toward him. Mike had a small company of about 90 employees. "Why would a union bother with such a small company?" he wondered. "Mr. Post", began Jeremy, "here's a notice saying that we will be having a yes or no vote on establishing a union in your company," as he handed Mike an envelope. "The vote will take place in 120 days". And with that, Jeremy turned around and walked back to his car.

"Great, one more thing to add on the heap", Mike mumbled. He opened the front door and walked briskly to the steps that led to his second-floor office. This was his sanctuary and it had become the place where he could feel safe and protected. His father had built it during a rare remodeling project. It had windows on one side that overlooked the ambulance bay and employee breakroom. It was furnished with a big cherry wood desk and bookcases. On one side of the room was an oblong conference table and chairs and on the wall behind the table were the oil portraits of his grandfather, father, and himself. A whiteboard filled the adjacent wall at the head of the conference table. On the other side of the office was a nice couch and the door to his private bathroom.

Mike plopped the envelope into his in-basket and sat down behind his desk. He swiveled around to watch the day and night shifts trade reports and go their respective ways. Tom Barkly, his shift manager, was, as usual, yelling at one of the EMTs about something. There was a group of guys over in a corner of the break area obviously having a lively discussion. "No doubt talking about this union thing" Mike thought. In 120 days, things will most likely be very different...how would he cope then? This could destroy everything his granddad and dad built. He spun back around as Jana came in with his morning coffee and mail.

Jana was a sharp gal. In her mid-forties and always well dressed, he had hired her as his administrative assistant even though her past work experience and education could have gotten her a better job. When he interviewed her, she had said she was looking for the right opportunity. "Whatever," he had thought, and proceeded to offer her the job. Last year she took the initiative to take over the sales and marketing, much to Mike's relief. In the 4 years she had been with him, she had never let him down. She had become someone he trusted and depended on. He toyed with the idea of discussing the union situation with her and decided to bring her into the loop. "Jana, are you aware of the guys considering allowing the union in? Jana replied, "Yes, and frankly, I am concerned for the company's survival if that happens." Mike wondered if she had any thoughts on what to do.

Jana knew the pressures Mike was under and she even detected a pattern of withdrawal and wondered if he was in the early stages of depression. She realized that if something drastic wasn't done soon that the company would spiral downward beyond repair. As she handed Mike his coffee, she pointed out a particular piece of direct mail to him. "Mike, I know the guys in this company. Last year they helped one of my friends with their business. They helped him resolve several issues and the last I heard his business had grown 35% over the previous year. You may want to look at their mailing. I think they can help us. How many days until the union vote? Mike muttered, "120". Taking in a deep breath she encouraged Mike to give the company consideration as the quickest option for a solution.

Mike nodded his acknowledgement to Jana and made a show of getting down to business hoping Jana would get the hint to leave. Of course, Jana picked up on the hint and quietly left the room. Mike looked at the mail piece she had put on top the mail pile. He had been thinking about getting some outside help but, he had so many areas in his business that were falling apart he questioned whether he could afford to bring in a whole team of consultants to fix things. He opened the mailing from Discovery Coaching. The first line was an attention getter:

Has Your Business Ceased to Be Fun?

Mike was hooked. He read the rest of the brochure that described how having a business coach was like professional athletes having coaches. They both needed coaches to help them personally improve their skills and abilities while developing a high-performance team. Mike thought about the issues with his employees, the union, new competition, and his struggle with getting up and coming to work. He was ready for about anything that could help, and he trusted

Jana's judgment. He punched in her extension number, "Jana", he said when she answered, "would you set up an appointment with the Discovery Coaching folks?" Then he added," The sooner the better". Jana was pleasantly surprised and made a quick call.

Chapter Two

CULTURE HAPPENS AND ENDURES

Jana led John Kessler into Mike's office and asked if she could sit in on the conversation which was okay with Mike. Mike shook John's hand and ushered him into his office. John's unimposing look and personal style was warm, and Mike immediately felt at ease. As they sat down John asked Mike for the company's background story. When Mike had finished, John asked why Mike had called Discovery. Mike described the issues and struggles the company was having. He talked about the impending union vote and the new competition coming into town. Then John wanted to know about how the company was doing financially. With some pride in his voice, Mike told John about his positive net income, how he kept costs down, and how they were able replace customers who left, keeping sales at a level place even in a mature market.

John paused, thinking about the research he had done before arriving. He knew it was a family company and after seeing the portraits on the wall he knew he had to follow his hunch.

John's next question threw Mike for a loop. "Who runs the company", John asked. Mike's first response was "I do, of course". John was ready for this; he knew the real answer but wanted Mike to see it for himself. John asked, "Then you would feel comfortable selling or closing the company and doing something else?" John paused for effect then continued, "or you would be willing to change the way you do business even if it meant you no longer were an ambulance company?

Mike sat back and thought. This company had been in the family for 50 years, how could he just dump it? He looked at the portraits on the wall above the conference table and deep inside him a voice whispered that he didn't fit the role that had befallen him.

John sensed the turmoil Mike was having and pressed his point forward. "How much influence do your grandfather and father still have when it comes to running your company?" Again, he paused, then added, "I can help you change the future of this company but, only if you are truly in charge of its destiny and take the responsibility for its direction."

The light bulb of enlightenment began to glow in Mike's head. He could see several ways his father and grandfather still influenced the company. He remembered his car ride to work when he was thinking about his grandfather saying, "fix it up, wear it out, make it do, or do without" and considered that might be what John was talking about.

He always had a fear that he wouldn't measure up to the way they had done things. At this point Mike was desperate enough to try anything. "I think I see your point. I have to be willing to change anything that doesn't work in today's reality. Is that it?"

"That's a good start, John answered. But, as a warning, change almost always requires painful decisions and the execution of those decisions. If I agree to be your coach, I will help you process a number of factors and emotions that will challenge your thinking, beliefs, and habits. That can be very hard for some people. Are you ready to commit to the kind of work it is going to take to turn things around?

In Mike's mind he weighed the alternatives. He could continue doing what he was doing and hope for different results. That approach was already causing a lot of anguish and pain and wearing him out. Or, he could choose to do something different and experience the kind of pain that had a better chance of producing positive results. Isn't this philosophy something he was always trying to impart to his students? Now that he was on the receiving end of those words, he was realizing it wasn't so easy to just flip that switch.

The costs of either alternative would be expensive, but the value and results would be far different. Mike was wondering if he really could make that shift. What would granddad and dad say? They would just laugh at John and his "weird" ideas. But they weren't facing the union or a new competitor. What if he gets started and just can't do it? That was ridiculous. He was an educator; there was nothing he couldn't learn and teach if he put his mind to it. Perhaps this was just the challenge he needed to become interested in the business. Mike looked at John and said, "Sure! How do we start?" "At the beginning", said John. "Let me explain it this way.

Imagine that your business is a train. The tracks that it runs on are critical to the train moving forward. One rail of the tracks is what I call "Operations". This is all the practical things like administration, procedures, processes, data flow, computers, sales, and marketing. In other words, it's the systems that you put in place to deliver your product to the customer.

The railroad ties that hold the two rails together represent "Leadership". Leadership is more than management, it provides direction, stability and makes the normally straight steel rails bend to make curves and avoid natural obstacles; in other words, agility. Leadership creates the strategies that allow the company to make the best use of its natural strengths and the opportunities it sees, defend against threats, and find workarounds for its weaknesses.

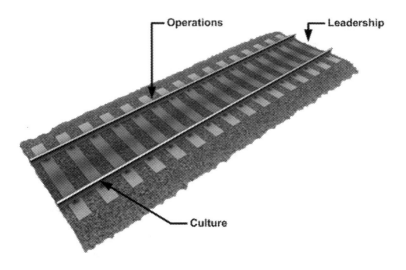

The second rail is "Culture". Every company needs people who do the work and deliver the product. Culture is the environment that those people work in. It includes values, vision, mission, and everything concerned with the relationships of employees, stakeholders, customers, and society. Culture always happens. It is either created by evolution or it is designed.

When one of the rails is shorter than the other it is inevitable that a train wreck will result. Now, many companies show success by having good Operations and Leadership. And because Culture "always happens" the train will continue to run. But, a company with a weak culture will experience a slower velocity of growth and likely, will not achieve its full potential. This is because when the Culture rail is weak or ineffective the train will derail on that side. "I'm guessing one of the core issues in your business centers around culture.

At this point, let me add that the first key to creating a strong Culture is to: Design Your Culture. The choice is clear; you are either proactive and design the Culture or it will design itself. The problem with the latter approach is that chaos is an unpredictable architect.

Design Your Culture

The symptoms of poor cultural design show up as high turnover of employees, discipline issues, lack of execution on directives, lack of innovation and creativity, customer retention issues, and plateau of growth. Sound familiar?" John asked.

"Sounds like everything we're experiencing", Mike responded, "but, I don't see how customer retention and plateau of growth fit in."

"Think about how your customers interact with your company. If the people they interact with are not fully engaged and in love with what they do your customers will sense that cue and it allows them to more easily leave your services[1.]. Growth happens when you are able to leverage your resources in a focused manner. However, when you are fighting on several battle fronts such as hiring and training new people, and other human resource issues you cannot bring enough focused resources or energy to bear on real strong growth."

Now John began to press his earlier statement that a core issue was centered on culture. He added, "You told me earlier about an imminent threat of unionization. If that happens, your sustainability will be impacted. And the union will inhibit your ability to combat the second threat of a new competitor coming into your market. These issues threaten the survival of your company or at least reduce its value if you want to sell.

So…we need to start by redesigning and changing your culture, so your people feel comfortable voting against the union. How many days before the vote?" Mike told him 120. John told him there was not a day to waste then. He said that would be the priority and later they could work on the competition issue."

This all made sense to Mike. But he was beginning to sense the enormity of the problems facing him and realizing the pain and work he would have to do to fix things. "The problem is so big; can we change it in time?" Mike mumbled.

Chapter Three

BALANCING ACT

"Now that you understand about Operations, Leadership, and Culture let's find out what drives them. Business courses in college teach that every business plan must have statements of Mission, Vision & Values." Of the companies that even have a business plan with these components, very few use them to their full advantage.

Mike thought about the last time he saw his business plan when he was trying to borrow capital from the bank two or three years ago. He remembered that it was in a storage closet where he kept the prior year's files. Embarrassed with those thoughts, he refocused on the teaching John was beginning to build. "Is there a relationship between Mission, Vision, and Values and Operations, Leadership, and Culture?"" queried Mike, feeling like a little kid searching for approval from the teacher.

"Absolutely", an astounded John exclaimed, "In your case, your mission is probably okay, your vision needs some adjustment for clarity, and you probably have never really deliberately defined your values. Now let's add one more set of pieces to the puzzle with the secret formula for a high-performance company".

Mike was perplexed. He had never thought about becoming a "high performance company", he had only wanted to fix some problems, get some sleep, and find his sanity again. How am I going to have a high-performance company? He felt twinges of fear and excitement.

John continued, "DO + BE = HAVE. Now, Mike, how does that relate to the words you've already heard?"

Mike went to the conference room whiteboard and wrote the words out:

"Well, DO probably fits with Operations and Mission. Is BE associated with Culture and Values? And, HAVE mean Leadership gets all the benefits?" "That's almost right", said John. "Leadership is the + sign. It is the joiner of DO and BE. HAVE are the results you get." Then John took over the whiteboard and put the plus sign in the right spot and added a column, so Mike's word matrix looked like this:

Management's responsibilities & focus	Operations	Leadership	Culture
Why employees are motivated –Purpose	Mission	Vision	Values
How each employee's character executes the Mission, Vision, and Values	DO	+	BE

John continued at the whiteboard and drew this picture for Mike.

"If your emphasis is on Operations then, at best, your HAVE will be average, and the full potential of the company is not reached. Too many resources will get sidetracked into maintaining the bureaucracy and support systems needed to prevent a meltdown of the internal structures.

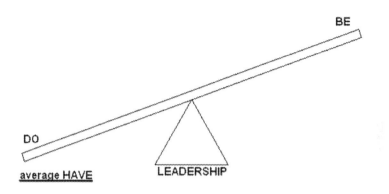

On the other hand, too much emphasis placed on the BE side is a worse fate for the business. The business may have great vacation and medical benefits and a latte lounge in each department, but the effect is worse than being over-focused on the DO side. The company's survival is at stake because Operations won't produce enough revenue.

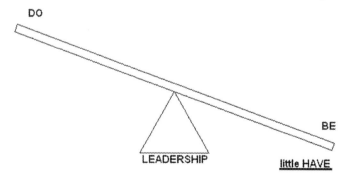

However, when you balance your focus between DO and BE an extraordinary synergy happens and an ABUNDANT HAVE results.

A company in this position will have more effective marketing and sales, a higher customer retention rate, less employee turnover so they will experience fewer training costs, and the atmosphere becomes more trusting and fun. Therefore, it takes less bureaucracy to run things. Finally, employees will probably be more productive and innovative leading to

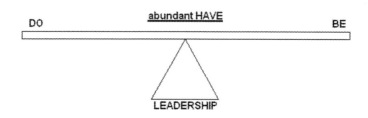

double digit growth in sales and in net profits. In other words— a high performance company.

There is one other thing piece I haven't mentioned about these diagrams", John said. "I said that DO and BE are joined by Leadership, in fact, Leadership is the fulcrum that everything balances on. The amount of the ABUNDANT HAVE is determined by the depth (or quality) of the Leadership. To continuously increase the company's level of success, Leadership must continuously improve itself[2]."

Mike's head was swimming with all he had just learned. He knew that he wanted to have an ABUNDANT HAVE and to do that he would have to work on his Leadership and Values to balance his Operations. The tangible expressions of these were the written mission, vision, and values documents. Could he pull all that together in time to avoid his company from unionizing or keep the new competition from coming in? His thoughts could have been telegraphed to John.

Leadership must continuously improve

John spoke, "If you are willing to work hard and make some painful decisions for a short period of time, I believe that we can make major progress towards solving the big issues you're facing within the next 30-60 days. Then we will work on tuning your organization to increase its velocity over the following 8 months or so."

Mike didn't know what John meant by the term "velocity" but, expected he would learn it when the time was right. "I think we've had enough for today" said John, "let me give you an assignment for homework and tomorrow we'll knock off some objectives."

ASSIGNMENT:

Write what the ideal working environment would look and feel like from:

    a.   Your point of view
    b.   Your employees' point of view
    c.   And your customers point of view

After John had left, Mike enthusiastically went to work on the assignment. He called Jana in to help him develop the wording of the different points of view. During that time he stopped and looked at Jana and said, "Jana do you really think we can pull this off?" Jana said, "Absolutely, but it will require some hard work and significant changes over the next few weeks and months." Mike said, "Yeah, that's what scares me." What did you think about all of the drawings and concepts John talked about today?"

Jana had been hoping Mike would ask her that very question. She took advantage of the opportunity and said, "Mike, do you remember when you interviewed me, and I told you I was just looking for an opportunity?" Mike said, "Yes, I was just thinking about that this morning before John arrived." Jana said, "After being here for 4 years, I know this is an incredible opportunity for me, but more importantly, I know that John is exactly right in what he was saying.

You have a great legacy and making changes as John is suggesting, can only make the legacy greater. I want to be a part of these changes and believe not only will the employees vote the union down, but the new competitor can be looked at as healthy competition and keep us on our toes. I say let's go for it and finish this assignment. Thanks for asking me to participate Mike." So, they focused on the assignment and here is what they came up with:

From My Point of View:

> People should enjoy coming to work. The pay scale would be an insignificant factor compared to the environment they get to work in. The environment would be safe, clean, and instill a pride in the people who work here. The managers would not have to use their titles as a club to get things done. Instead, work gets done because the team wants to achieve great things. We would encourage people to share their ideas for improving the company. There would not be a "them vs. us" atmosphere instead; we would be a team with everybody playing their respective role.

From My Employees of View:

> Being paid well is secondary to the joy I have when I come to work. I want to feel very confident that I'm doing my best and I'm naturally great at doing my job. In fact, I have superb performance. I want to know that my boss cares about me and is encouraging me. I want to be challenged and not get into a rut. I want to be energized and look forward to coming in to work. I want my ideas to be heard and considered. I want to feel valued, respected, and rewarded for my exceptional efforts. And everybody benefits from the company's success.

From My Customers of View:

> We want to feel valued and that we are getting the best value for
> the dollars we spend with your company. We want to trust that
> there is nothing that will stand in the way of the best quality
> of service—because our lives often depend on it. We expect
> professionalism and confidence from those who touch us and
> assurance that they have the latest equipment and training.

Mike left work reluctantly. He was anxious to see what was
possible in his old company and wondered about John's early question
about the influence his predecessors still had on the company. He
was newly determined that if their influence was negatively affecting
his "high performance company" that those traditions would die.

Jana left work excited but a bit apprehensive in thinking about
what challenges lay ahead for Mike. She was hopeful he would be
able to let go of the "old ways of thinking," and embrace the new
concepts John was talking about. This business could be the top
requested ambulance service soon. Jana pulled out of the parking
lot feeling great about the day and looking forward to the meeting
tomorrow.

Chapter Four

GHOSTS DIE HARD

Mike didn't sleep well again however, this time it was from the excitement of what might be possible. As he arrived at work, he was thinking that Jana had been great at helping him complete the assignment the day before. He thought she might be valuable today working with he and John as another pair of eyes and ears.

Jana had prepared for the day's meeting with John with carafes of coffee, breakfast quiche, and fruit. Mike was impressed but not surprised. "Jana", he said, "if it is possible with your schedule I was wondering if you would like to join our discussions today? I could use another set of smarts to help me absorb and work on everything." Jana appreciated the compliment and had been hoping he would ask her.

Just then John knocked on the office door. Mike invited him in and asked if it was okay that Jana joined them again. Now, John had met Jana when she worked at one of his previous clients. He had done strengths and behavior profiles on her at that time, and knew she had the right stuff to be a core team member and a leader so; he welcomed her aboard as a co-conspirator.

John outlined his short-term strategy, "because your issue with the union is so pressing, we are going to limit our focus on one value and several principles required to anchor it in your business. It will be enough to get you started and will take some time to complete. However, it will provide the basis for taking action and changing some critical areas."

"We'll start with the value. Show me what you wrote for your assignment." Mike handed John a copy of the paragraphs he and Jana had worked the night before. "Please note", began John, "that when you describe the environment that it is centered on the relationships between customers, employees, and management. How you treat people, what your behavior is, the integrity of what you say and do are all part of the essence of the term BE. So, to give you a kick start on the list of values you'll develop later, I'm going to suggest one that I believe should be universal for all businesses." John went to the whiteboard and wrote:

TRUSTWORTHY

"Trust is a firm reliance on the integrity, ability, or character of a person. Worthy is having sufficient value or importance. Together they mean that a person is deserving of trust or confidence; dependable; reliable:

"Your grandfather and father founded and ran this company during a time in our history where employees respected or feared the boss. Command and control was the style of management that worked for that time. Tell me about how you motivate your employees."

"I use the carrot and stick method", Mike said, rather proud that he could draw on his teaching background as well as using a term his father used.

John: "So, how has that been working for you?

Mike felt resistance to John's question. If the carrot and stick worked for his dad and granddad it should work for him…after all, this company would not have reached its level of success if his dad and granddad had not been good managers.

Mike spoke up, "the employees want strong leadership; they respect a 'take charge' guy. And, if they sense weakness, they'll run all over the manager. They can trust that they will get paid, and I've never missed a payroll."

Sensing the raw emotions coming to the surface, John pressed the issue, "Is that how you saw your dad manage? Do you think the union issue may have its roots in lack of trust?"

Mike's voice elevated in intensity, "What does the carrot and stick have to do with trust? And how would that relate to the union issue?"

John responded, "your grandfather and father learned management skills during the industrial age. That culture had different values; management science and psychology were still a long way from maturity. The carrot and stick management methods were based on conditioning theory developed during observations by Ivan Pavlov in his experiments on dog's digestion. However, humans tend to resent being 'conditioned'.

Trust is built on actions that employees hope to see.

Today, we are transitioning into a new age. The people working today have different values from those 60 years ago. They are more independent and self-aware than in the past. Management science and psychology has greatly matured and now you must know how to lead people instead of managing them.

Making payroll is only a small portion of how trust is built, and it is really the expected condition of the agreement you have with your employees. Trust is built on your actions that employees hope to see.

They hope the company cares about them personally; they hope the company will recognize their work; they hope they will have the right tools to do the job; they hope to enjoy their work and make friends; they hope the environment is pleasant; they hope the work is challenging and provides opportunities.

Your assignment was to describe what the ideal working environment would look and feel like from:

    a. Your point of view
    b. Your employees' point of view
    c. And your customers point of view

In order to achieve that environment what you say must align with what you do. If you tell employees that we need to cut expenses and then buy new furniture for your office then you have lost integrity and trust.

From reading over your assignment I'd say you are on the right track for how the future could be. However, the ghosts of the past will not allow you to move into the vision of what you want. They are signals of the past and they chain you to the past.

You need new signals that direct the best of what your company can be."

The light bulb in Mike's head clicked on. And his immediate question to john was, "Tell me more about 'signals'."

John again went to the whiteboard and wrote SIGNALING above TRUSTWORTHY and then drew an arrow.

SIGNALING

TRUSTWORTHY

Let's compare what trust produces against a lack of trust. Then we can begin to understand the principal of signaling"

Chapter Five

THE SHIFT

John produced a document he had prepared earlier. "Look at this table and let's see how you think your company would rate on a trust scale."

Put an 'x' in the box to the right of the statement that best matches your company			
Established TRUST produces:		**Lack of TRUST produces:**	
Communications that transform people positively		Hidden or limited communications	
Employee feels that management is approachable with any issue		Employee feels that management is not approachable and may even lean towards sabotaging behaviors	
Employee alignment		Employee personal agendas	
High productivity		Average productivity	

Regular creative and innovative ideas		Sporadic innovation	
Energized workplace atmosphere		Sluggish workplace atmosphere	
High customer retention		Low customer retention	
People care about quality, customers, and the company		People are there for the paycheck and look out for themselves	
Few policies and controls needed to control employee drama and issues		More time, energy, money is applied to control employee drama and issues	
Capital resources are available and directed towards growth		Capital resources are siphoned towards bureaucracy	
Add the number of 'x's in the first column→		Add the number of 'x's in the second column and multiply by 4→	
Subtract the second column from the first→			

Jana shook her head when mike replied with a negative number of 20. "Mike, get real", she began, "don't you see that unionizing is a form of sabotage? I think we are more like a negative 35. Many of the ambulance drivers are only here because of the paycheck for relatively easy workload. And when was the last time you heard real laughter around here?"

Mike's shoulders sank and his head bowed down. He knew Jana was right and he was just lying to himself. The impact of the last fifteen minutes fully landed on him and he knew change was at hand.

"What can we do to change the level of trust?" he asked. "And why are the negative x's multiplied by 4?" John answered the last question first, "The short answer is that it takes 4 or 5 positive signals to offset just 1 negative signal[16.]. We'll talk more about that later, but for now let's talk about changing the level of trust."

"We identify as many anti-trust signals in your company and work toward changing those. Remember I said that trust is built on actions that employees hope to see. The union promises actions that fulfill their hope. We will replace the anti-trust signals with ones that provide better alternatives than the union.

John added, "Now that you understand why trust is important, we can discuss how signaling builds trust.

Signaling is about how your employees perceive the "truth" in your company. It happens through the things you do, the conditions of the work environment, the unspoken "rules" of how to behave among other artifacts your company collects. It is either positive or negative according to their perceptions. And, if you aren't deliberate about thinking through your signals, you will send conflicting signals.

Remember I said that trust is built on your actions that employees hope to see; positive signals fuels positive trust.

For instance, if you want people to share their ideas for improving the company you need to develop an atmosphere where they can safely share without fear of reprimand or derision. A suggestion box will never cut it in today's workplace. Or, if you need the team to put in extra hours to knock out a project then they need to see you make a sacrifice too.

Signaling is the alignment of what leadership professes as values, beliefs, policies, or anything that is stated and its actions, decisions, behavior, symbols, or words. If leadership says one thing but demonstrates by their actions something else, then trust is lessoned. Therefore, signaling is the expression of the leader's integrity.

> **Signaling Expresses Quality of Integrity**

Consistent Positive Signals Builds Trust

Signaling with purpose can turn around an organization quickly however; trust comes only as people see consistency of signals over time. Research shows that it takes 4 or 5 positive signals to offset just 1 negative signal. Therefore a leader must make sure his staff understand what the signals are and carry them out without personal prejudice.

Let's make a list of possible negative signals. From the little time I've been here I have observed several."

Mike watched as Jana went to the board and immediately began writing under the heading of:

NEGATIVE SIGNALS

- Mike's private office with cherry wood and portraits of past company presidents
- Private office bathroom
- Office overlooks the ambulance bay and employee break area.

Anticipating Mike's question Jana spoke, "the office is a symbol of control and authority. It is intimidating to most people who work here. The signal is 'them vs. us'. The same reason applies to these next items:"

- Disengagement of Mike from the employees.
- The poor condition of the ambulances and the EMT's equipment.

Not wanting a coaching opportunity to slip by John asked Mike for more understanding on how the condition of the vehicles and equipment had gotten so poor.

"I suppose it's the words of my grandfather about 'fix it up, wear it out, make it do, or do without' that has guided me. Mike paused, then said. "Is that another ghost?"

John nodded and added, "In this case, it is a belief that is sending the wrong signal. What does it say about your company when the public sees a rusty ambulance or old poorly functioning equipment picking up or delivering a patient?" Somewhere in their mind they may have the thought that you don't care, and that can lose business.

How do your employees perceive the condition? If you don't care, will they still care as much as they should?

John added his short list:

- Reserved parking space.
- People in the organization who are saboteurs of change.
- Lack of fresh vision, promoted values.

Mike was nodding in agreement and finally added his own ideas to the list:

- Letting Tom Barkly run everything
- Not involving more people in decision making.

John then asked the question of what action could be taken to offset the negatives. Mike interrupted by suggesting they bring in some others into this session to help.

"That's a good first step towards re-engaging with the employees" John affirmed. "Who do you suggest?"

When Mike brought up the name of his supervisor, Tom Barkly. Jana reacted, "I don't think he is the kind of person who will respond well," she offered.

Mike replied, "Let's give him a chance, would you go ask him to come up please? And, on the way, brief him on what we are doing."

Meanwhile Mike and John began writing their thoughts on how to offset some of the negatives.

Chapter Six

TOUGH DECISION

Tom walked in the room and introductions were made. John sensed arrogance about Tom right away but continued to explain what they have been doing and adding that his input was important. "Let's get back to board and review the negative signals list and start listing the actions we can do to turn things around" John said.

POSITIVE SIGNALS

- Turn the reserved parking space into one for Employee of the Month…
- Tom jumped in, "What about shift manager parking or manager of the month?""

Good thought" John responded, "let's keep going on the list and then we can discuss options and insights we have."

- Begin mingling with employees during shift changes; ask questions; give them latitude to express opinions, ideas, and suggestions.

Tom had a puzzled look on his face.

- Set up scheduled employee meetings for input and feedback on progress with ideas and suggestions.

Tom's puzzled look began turning into a frown and his head began shaking.

- Move Mike's office downstairs and turn his current office into the break/meeting room for the employees.

With his frustration now obvious, Tom spoke, "Why do you want to spend good money on that? They won't appreciate it." Your dad would have never spent money like that. Seems to me, you are giving up control to the employees because you don't want the union coming in…what good will come from that?"

John responded quickly, "keep that thought Tom; we need to continue and capture our positive ideas for now."

- Invest in new equipment and thoroughly repair or replace our fleet.

Tom turned silent and the frown deepened… seeing his bonus disappearing.

- Weed out incorrigible employees who undermine leadership direction.

Jana jumped on the last point first and suggested that they make an individual list of positives and negatives for each employee and then compare them. Mike wasn't sure he knew enough about the employees to do that.

John asked Tom how he feels about developing that list and Tom responded, "I don't think it's important that that we need a list like that." John replied, "Okay, instead, let's come up with a set of criteria that you want employees to have and then sees who best fits into those criteria."

Jana liked this idea better, Mike was also more comfortable with it, and Tom went back to silence. Jana took the initiative to go up to the white board and finding some open space she wrote:

EMPLOYEE CRITERIA GOING FORWARD

- Open-minded
- Good judgment
- Critical thinker
- Trustworthy
- Self-control (disciplined)

John said, "Great! Now focus on the behaviors of each one of your employees with respect to this list. Can you think of times these qualities have been demonstrated?"

Tom blurted out, "We won't have anyone left working for us if this is what we look for. Ain't nobody that's that good. That's why I'm always having to whip em into shape."

An agitated Jana, barely keeping her emotions in check, replied, "And while you're whipping them into shape, your voice gets loud and almost abusive, Tom. Is that really the best way to get the results you are looking for? To be honest with you, I've had some comments made to me about how your treat people on your shift."

"Who's been whining to you?" Tom's voice elevated in intensity, "Why didn't you send them to me or tell me about it? I would have nipped that right in the bud."

Mike sensed Tom's temper starting to flair and took the opportunity to intervene, "Tom, don't get upset...we are not here to attack you, we're here to rethink some things."

Tom is now clearly dismayed at how the conversation is turning. "Mike I just don't see why anything has to change. Man, everything was fine when your dad ran things." Mike took a deep breath...

John stepped in before Mike could unload on Tom. "Tom let's consider what Mike is saying. We think the old management style of bringing employees into compliance through incentives and intimidation is going away. There is a whole new generation in the workplace today that doesn't respond well to being commanded what to do. What worked well yesterday doesn't mean it will work well today. That style is passing away and a more team-oriented workforce is taking its place.

This requires that managers become more like coaches and facilitators and the workforce participates more. Frankly, this reduces stress on everybody. You might like this much better."

Tom grumbled, "I don't know nothing else. I like the way things are."

John knew at this point that Tom was not going to adapt to any change but, as a coach, Mike and Jana would have to reach their own conclusions. John spoke carefully, "Tom, being forthright is commendable. And, obviously Mike and Jana value your input, so let's try to move forward. Tell me Tom, who on your shift can be mentored by you to become this type of employee and become a leader?"

Tom still clearly disturbed said. "I don't know, I have never looked at my shift this way. They are just employees here to perform a service and collect a paycheck. As long as they show up and do their job why would I want more? That works for me and it always worked with Mike's dad."

Mike had calmed down and said, "Tom I appreciate your loyalty to my dad and this business, but dad isn't here anymore. The business is struggling to move forward and we need to do something different if we want better results. I really need you to work on this with us. I know your shift is over and you need to get out of here, so why don't you take off, think about John's question, and we will meet again tomorrow."

John took the opportunity to close this part of the meeting and addresses Tom, "That's a good idea. So Tom, your assignment for tonight is to think about those people who can be mentored to become the type of employees we've identified. Thanks for joining us and we'll talk again tomorrow." Tom got up, "Yeah, yeah...see ya." and left quickly.

After Tom closed the door, Jana bursts out, "I said earlier that I had concerns about including Tom in this meeting. Now I am glad we did. Do you see it Mike?"

Mike is thoughtful and fearful about what he is about to say. "Well, I am pretty disappointed. Maybe he is the first person we need to measure against this criteria list; although, I think the red flags are everywhere."

"Well, why don't we do that?" Jana said. John is now much more confident about Mike and Jana's ability to make the tough decisions.

Mike continued, "Tom has been with us for almost 22 years. Dad thought he was great and that's why he promoted him to manager of the shift. But every morning I look down into that room and watch Tom verbally beating our people and, until today, I thought it was expected from the manager, even though it bothered me. After working on the assignment last night and listening to him during this meeting, it is not okay. Measuring Tom against these criteria, I would say he falls short in every point. Is that how you see it, Jana?"

"Mike, I'm relieved that you see Tom's shortcomings. The changes we are making are exciting and I have no doubt they will put us back on track. Tom will block us with every move. I think we need to let him go and quickly. That decision means we must have a replacement for him immediately. So, let's review the employees against the criteria and find the best choice. We don't have time to look outside of the organization right now."

John interrupts and says, "you are headed in a good direction. I suggest that you take this one step at a time and evaluate your employees first. If you find a gap in your staff that requires looking outside, we can deal with that later."

Mike and Jana agree to evaluate the employees as best they can. John suggests, "you might consider adding an additional quality such as 'influencer'. The person replacing Tom needs to have influential authority as opposed to positional authority."

With the 1st shift over, John's growling stomach prompts him to suggest they can go to lunch and discuss the positive signals list they didn't get to earlier and some ideas on how to communicate the shifting direction of the company.

On the way, they discuss several people who could take Tom's place and land on Robert Baker the 2nd shift manager. The conclude that Robert should help decide who would take his place. The decision about Tom is made and they will talk to Tom after discussing the changes with Robert.

Chapter Seven

ACTIONS AND VULNERABILITY

Jana called Robert and asked him to come in an hour before his shift started. Robert agreed and began to fear that he might be demoted or terminated. Wonder what Tom Barkly said to them, he thought. What was he going to do if they fired him? How would he tell his wife? They just bought their new home and are expecting their second child. Well, there is that new competitor opening soon. I can talk to them. I know the market and even has some ideas how to gain some customers. At least I have a shift of guys who trust me. Maybe tomorrow after work I'll stop off at the competitor's office and just talk to them.

In the morning Mike arrived looking refreshed, energized, and ready for the day. He dropped a box on the break table downstairs and said a loud "Good morning!" to the employees. There were a few mumbled responses. Someone opened the box and it was filled with all types of pastries. Jana smiled. Way to go Mike! Then she heard someone say, "Guess he's trying to kill us off so we won't vote for the union. A low laugh rumbled through the warehouse bay. Tom chuckled but then told everyone to be quiet and get moving. "Grab a donut and get busy," He said.

Robert walked into the building and Tom was the first person he saw. Robert thought Tom had a nasty look on his face. Must have been a bad day again. Wonder who caught his tongue lashing today. That kind of stuff is why they all want the union in so bad. Seems like the only option, though, too bad for Mike's business.

Before Robert could speak, Tom curtly asked, "Why are you here so early? Wanting to make sure I do things right?" Robert has no idea what prompted that kind of question, but said, "Hey Tom. Nope, I got a call from Jana last night and the boss wanted to see me."

Tom said, "Oh yeah, they probably want to tell you all about some employee criteria crap. They brought me in on that yesterday. Just something their consultant is filling their head with. I wouldn't worry about it. Since Mike's not involved much, we can just keep doing what we're doing. No one will even notice. Good luck."

Robert calmed down a bit and his curiosity now spiked his thinking. Wonder what Mike is changing. Is this just a ploy to head off the unionization? This will be interesting…

Robert knocked on the door and Mike yelled, "Come on in." Opening the door, Robert saw Mike and Jana sitting at the conference table and the whiteboard filled with all types of words and drawings. They greet each other and Mike told Robert to grab a snack and something to drink and have a seat. Wow! This is something new, Robert thought. Mike is doing some serious buttering up.

Mike started the conversation by telling Robert that he has not been happy in the company or the direction it was going. He had found himself becoming more disengaged and pulling further away from the leadership role. He now realizes that he was more the problem than anyone or any situation facing the company.

Mike continued explaining to Robert about the company's status, the competition, what he wants to do, and some of the action steps that he wants to take. He also showed Robert the document that envisioned the "ideal working environment" and explained the different points from:

- My Point of View
- My Employees of View
- My Customers of View

Robert's mind was spinning with excitement and all kinds of ideas he would like to lay out to Mike but, he didn't know how much he should trust what was being said.

Before Robert could contribute anything, Mike says, "So all of this brings me to the reason Jana and I asked you to come in early today. We evaluated many of the employees against the criteria on the board. The conclusion we came to is that you are the person who meets the criteria and demonstrates the ability to embrace change and collaborate with Jana and I to develop the team we want here. Would you consider taking the 1st shift manager position Robert?"

Robert was stunned! These were the last words he expected to hear today. Would he? "You bet! Robert replied, "I'd love the opportunity to be on the ground floor helping to implement these changes and developing the culture you talked about. I have a lot of ideas myself when you are ready to hear them."

Suddenly, Robert realized the position they were talking about was Tom's position. What did that mean? Robert had to ask, "Mike, what happens to Tom? Will he take over my shift? I have some concerns about that."

Mike assured Robert that was not the case and some initial changes would be made immediately. Jana said, "Robert, what we would like is for you to review the employees with us and determine who your replacement should be." Robert thought about the confidence they were placing in him. He said, "Absolutely, I'm ready to get started."

For the next thirty minutes the three of them discussed the employees based on the criteria listed on the whiteboard. Mike and Jana were impressed with Robert's intuitiveness, practicality, fairness, and transparency. He really did know the employees. Seeing Robert's animation and engagement was a relief to both Jana and Mike and 180 degrees from Tom's reaction. Robert had to get ready for his team to come in, so they let him go. Robert helped them narrow the options down to two people as his replacement before leaving for the shift change. Now it was up to Mike and Jana.

One of the choices was Susan. She had been with the company as long as Jana. The other choice was Charlie and he had been with the company for 3 years. Jana felt like Susan was the better choice because she fit the criteria almost as well as Robert did; perhaps not quite as much of an influencer though.

Mike, on the other hand, felt like Charlie was the better choice even though he could get agitated at times about some of the team members performance. He thought Charlie was good at influencing and they would need someone with that ability.

Jana conceded but still voiced her reservations that Charlie could end up being more like Tom if the employees didn't immediately come around. So, the decision was made to promote Charlie.

Once the shift change was completed and the day slowed down, Robert came back to work with Mike and Jana. Next on Mike's agenda was to discuss the signals that had been identified and talk about what could be done to address them. Jana had put them in document form and handed a copy to Mike. The compilation looked like this:

	Negative Signals	**Positive Signals**
1.	Mike's private office with cherry wood and portraits of past company presidents	Move Mike's office downstairs. Put the portraits in storage
2.	Private office bathroom	See above. Becomes an employee bathroom

3.	Office overlooks the ambulance bay and employee break area.	Turn Mike's old office into the break/meeting room for the employees. Remove the glass panes separating the activity
4.	Disengagement of Mike from the employees.	Begin mingling with employees during shift changes; show care by asking questions; encourage expressions of opinions, ideas, and suggestions.
5.	The poor condition of the ambulances and the EMT's equipment.	Change Mike's belief about equipment. Invest in new equipment and thoroughly repair or replace our fleet.
6.	Reserved parking space.	Turn the reserved parking space into one for Employee of the Month or just normal parking
7.	People in the organization who are saboteurs of change.	Weed out incorrigible employees who undermine leadership direction.
8.	Lack of fresh vision, promoted values.	Create a core team that is willing to discuss, challenge, and make decisions together
9.	Letting Tom Barkly run everything	???

10.	Not involving more people in decision making.	Set up scheduled employee meetings for input and feedback on progress with ideas and suggestions.

The team discussed how Tom's departure would begin to set the tone for the changes coming and that all the negative areas should be addressed at the same time.

Robert suggested that the EMT uniforms did not represent the company well since they tended to be in poor shape and cleanliness tended to be an issue. Also, he thought it was another thing that made the employees feel less proud of where they worked.

Jana said that she would look into a uniform service. Then, changing the subject, she added that single acts of signal changing would probably not reverse the negative trust score. She reminded Mike and Robert what John had said about consistent positive signals building trust. She emphasized the fact that it took 4 or 5 positive signals to offset just 1 negative signal.

Together they tried to figure out what other things they could do to increase the number of positive signals but didn't come up with much and decided to ask John about it when he came back.

Mike thought about John's reaction when he came in tomorrow and hear how much had already been accomplished. The next step was to terminate Tom. They agreed to do that first thing before tomorrow's morning shift started and have Robert come in to get the shift underway.

This next day Jana came in early to prepare for the meeting with John. She wondered how Mike would handle the inevitable confrontation with Tom. This would be a true test of his courage and determination to make the changes and let go of the past.

When Tom came in for the shift, Mike called him upstairs and asks Jana to come into the office as well. In the meantime, Robert showed up and prepared the shift to keep things moving. Everyone was puzzled and wondering what was going on. In a few minutes the door to Mike's office slammed shut, Tom stomped down the stairs and went straight to his locker. Mike and Jana came out the door immediately and down the stairs just in time to see Tom gather everything in his locker, slam the door shut, and yell, "Later, losers," as he walked out. Everyone just stared in stunned silence. Robert said, "Okay everyone, I believe Mike and Jana have some things to talk to us about. Let's all take a seat."

Mike asked everyone to relax and began to explain what had just happened. "We are going to be making some changes over the next few months and unfortunately, Tom did not wish to be a part of those changes. Robert has agreed to step up and help by taking the manager position and we are asking Charlie to take over Robert's shift. I hope you will all cooperate with them and get excited about what is happening." After a moment to let that sink in, Mike continued:

"I would like to apologize to all of you for being an absentee owner and basically not being involved in making things right with the business.

The timing for making these changes is long overdue. I must admit that the pressure from the union got me to thinking about this, along with another competitor coming into the market. And, frankly, I did not look forward to coming in to work; it had ceased to be fun.

This forced me to think about the survival of the business. Some of you may be thinking I am just doing this to try and sway the union vote. But I have retained a business coach who has assured me that we can turn the company around, be highly competitive, and get back to being the best ambulance service in this area.

When John started the coaching process with me, he helped me understand that I am the cause of most of the problems the business is facing right now. My thinking was haunted by the ghosts of my father and grandfather and we have committed to retire the past and find the right balance for how we are going to build our business together. This will no longer be my father's or grandfather's business. It is our business. So, I hope you will help me make this transition.

Gary spoke up, "So does this mean you are going to bring us donuts every morning?"

"Good question but, this is not about buying your votes" Mike said, "so donuts are unlikely to be on the table every morning." Most of the employees chuckled at the humor and the surprise that Mike could be personable. He continued, "But your input is valuable. We need to hear it and process it. Some ideas will probably be put into play and some won't be.

The first action we are taking is to improve safety and our image. To that end I'm asking for volunteers from each shift to go through each ambulance and make a list of what equipment we need to upgrade, add, and which ambulances should be repaired or replaced.

We need all-hands to help make this a great place to work. Folks this is just for starters and hopefully the other changes we've identified will be positive for most of you. This has been a long time coming and again, I apologize for neglecting the business and you."

Mike looked out at the employees and saw some who were excited, some unreadable and a more than a few skeptics. He thought, the new Mike was almost having fun and at the same moment he realized the work ahead would cost him.

He just didn't realize what how high the cost would be.

Chapter Eight

A GOOD START

At the coaching session that day John heard Mike and Jana tell about the events that had transpired thus far. Occasionally, John would interrupt to get a little more clarification and was also making some notes. When they came to the end of their story telling, john spoke.

"Let's make sure we affirm what we have learned about signaling so far using today's events as our base.

First let me commend you on getting Robert in here right away and for talking with the employees as a group. Remember, our actions must align with our words to build trust in our employees by meeting the hope of what they wish to see. Let's break down the signaling you have already used.

1. Talking with employees:

    - Your <u>Words</u> were the ones of taking personal responsibility.
    - Your <u>Action</u> was expressing that to Robert and the group.
    - The <u>Signal</u> to them was humility and getting involved.
    - The <u>Hope</u> is that change might still be possible.

2. Vision casting to Robert

- Your <u>Words</u> were shown in the document of how you saw what the company should look and feel like.
- Your <u>Action</u> was explaining the document to Robert.
- The <u>Signal</u> to him was your involvement and his.
- The <u>Hope</u> for Robert is involvement in the company's direction and outcomes. (You sent a reinforcing signal by asking him to help select his successor.)

Now let's talk about Tom's termination. In our discussion with Tom, he clearly signaled that he would not be comfortable with the new direction and style of management that was being created.

The Gallup Organization has categorized three categories of employees[1]:

1. Engaged— Go beyond job requirements - look for how to do more
2. Not Engaged— Do their job well - look forward to Friday and payday
3. Actively Disengaged— Do their job - look for ways to complain or undermine authority

Tom was somewhere between two and three. He gave indicators that he would slip into category three pretty quick and would begin to undermine and sabotage your efforts.

When employees are at catagory 3 they are very hard to pull back and the quicker you can get them 'off the bus' the better for the organization. Those people are cancerous and actively try to infect others to their way of thinking. So let's look at the signal you sent.

3. Tom's termination.

- Your <u>Words</u> were implied in the talk with the employees; that change was coming, and you only wanted people on the bus who wanted to be there and you will take the actions needed to make the changes.
- Your <u>Action</u>, of course, was firing Tom. But his exit theatrics also sent a signal to the onlookers that confirmed a good decision.
- The <u>Signal</u> is management's commitment to change direction regardless of a person's status or tenure.
- The <u>Hope</u> is that change may create a better environment.

Finally, you invited the employees to be part of the solution. Here's how that breaks down:

4. Employees as part of the solution

- Your <u>Words</u> were asking for their input.
- Your <u>Action</u> was asking for volunteers to evaluate the company equipment.
- The <u>Signal</u> to them is your trust for their input, and you are committing to improve working conditions.
- The <u>Hope</u> is for improved working conditions and pride in where they work.

Overall, you sent three positive signals to the employees that change for the better is coming. Of course, you will have to send out many more signals like that to prove your intentions.

One thing we haven't mentioned before, is that sometimes we send signals that have unintended consequences. So, in order to Design our Culture we follow a pattern that deliberately structures our signals that allows us to observe, measure, and tweak results.

Many companies follow a pattern of seeing a problem, finding a solution to that problem, and implementing the solution. The unintended

Anticipate Unintended Consequences

consequences tend to break something that seems unrelated to the first issue. Then they begin looking for a solution for the new issue and the cycle starts again.

For instance, take a company that wants to sell more widgets, so they offer cash incentives to their sales force and special incentives if they hit their sales goal for that month. For the next six months sales continually are higher but, then sales stop increasing, and they start looking for a justification as to why this is happening.

The unintended consequences are that the sales force was so focused on getting the next sale that customers felt like they were not important, so they either buy only one-time or go to another source next time. Also, maybe the sales force didn't take the time to process orders correctly so the fulfillment team must slow down or makes mistakes and fulfillment slowed down. Again, this can affect customer retention. And, when you have to replace customers you will spend more on marketing and sales activities.

Unintended signals are known to stifle productivity, innovation, and creativity. They can slow processes down, speed up employee and customer turnover requiring more costs to replace and train people. It becomes a vicious cycle. Unfortunately, most company owners see it as a normal cost of doing business. But I assure you it does not need to be that way.

That is why it is critical to design our cultural signals with structured intentions. That means to follow the pattern below.

1. Signal Conceived —you know you want to create or change something, and you have a plan for achieving the desired outcome.

2. Dry Test for Side Effects—this is an additional step that most managers skip because usually they are naturally self-assured

and assume their plan will work. Usually it does work but, unanticipated side-effects happen that break something else down the line.

3. Action (Signal Sent) —the signal is sent, and results begin to happen.

4. Measure Results —results are not limited to financial or statistical metrics. Results must be observed from a behavioral standpoint also.

5. Uncover Unexpected Results —changing behavior patterns can produce unexpected results. Many times, unexpected results don't show up until much later.

6. Tweak Original Communication —the natural tendency of management is to fix the unexpected results because they don't connect those with the first action they took. Instead they implement a new "fix" that tends to amplify or create additional problems. The answer is to fix the original communication, so the behavior doesn't have that side effect.

When you add steps 2 and 5 to your signal construction model, the management and administration costs cease to compound, and you increase the velocity needed to break into the next level. If you do not add those steps or are casual about your communication signals you can expect effects similar to the old children's song, "There's a Hole in My Bucket" which is based on a dialogue between Henry and Liza about a leaky bucket:

> *Liza needs the lazy Henry to fetch some water. But Henry tells Liza he has a leaky bucket, and Liza tells him to fix it. But to fix the leaky bucket, he needs straw. To cut the straw, he needs a knife. To sharpen the knife, he needs to wet the sharpening stone. To wet the stone, he needs water. Henry then asks Liza how to get the water, and her answer is "in a bucket". But, the bucket, if it could carry water, would not need repairing in the first place.*

Jana and Mike were now beginning to understand the power of signaling. But Mike heard the word velocity again and it was pricking his interest in how that applied to running a business. Mike asked John that very question.

John answered, "velocity refers to an object's rate of position change over a specific time period. For a business this means how quickly the business can move from point A to point B.

There are always natural forces at work that are constraints to movement. For instance, if we want to put a rocket into orbit, the rocket must overcome gravitational forces and friction by achieving an "escape velocity". They do this in stages. The first stage builds momentum, but the cost in fuel is huge. When the first stage has used up its fuel, they drop it away to reduce weight and friction so the second stage can be effective. With less weight, the next stage achieves the "escape velocity" for the payload to be delivered into space.

For an organization to move to the next level of maturity they need to achieve a similar type of velocity in stages; the first gets them to being operationally and financially good; the second stage builds to launch their company to being great.

Without firing up their second stage they will not be able to break through the constraints that hold them back and they continue to bump along the top of their ceiling – having success and being good enough but, never becoming great.

Two other common terms that illustrate the velocity principle are: "tipping point" or "critical mass". They each indicate the point at which significant change is not only probable it is almost certain.

So now let's spend the rest of this session talking about the next steps over the 90 day period and see if we can't stop unionization and then take on the completion."

Chapter Nine

CONFLICTING SIGNALS

Over the next 30 days John visited each week. On the second visit he found some of the staff struggling. A perplexed Jana explained, "The volunteers made up a list of equipment that the ambulances needed and the cost was around $8,000. One of the first items listed was several new fire extinguishers at a cost of $120. Mike questioned the need for new ones and asked why it couldn't just be recharged. The team explained but, Mike still was adamant about the expense. However, two days later he went out and spent $280 on a coffee/cappuccino machine for the employees. He thinks it will be a great moral booster for the employees. Robert and I think it sends the wrong signal."

Jana continued unloading on John, "I overheard Charlie bad-mouthing Mike and some of the changes in the direction of the business to others on the shift. I shared this with Mike because it seemed like what an Actively Disengaged employee would say, and he is the leader of that shift. But mike just blew me off and excused the behavior. I was so mad; he talks about making changes but instead backs away on the difficult issues. Which way does he want it?"

John was anticipating issues like this coming up. In fact, he was hopeful that even more would show up to create more teachable moments.

To maximize the moment, he asked Robert and Jana to join his session with Mike. "Mike", John started, "we have a fantastic opportunity to explore a signaling event that is currently in front of us." Mike shifted uneasily in his chair. Continuing, John said," I understand that the people who were given responsibility to develop a list of items needed, requested new fire extinguishers and you rejected their explanation of why it couldn't be recharged and declined the request based on cost."

Mike nodded and thought that was a reasonable decision. Now, John pressed his point, "you may have saved $120 dollars but, what was the cost in employee trust when you align what you said the other week with this action. That cost is much higher than the $120 saved. Did one of the ghosts of the past trick you into a bad decision?

Mike's stomach got a hollow burning sensation as he saw what John was saying. His next thought was had he ruined the all they had been working toward. Did they have to start again? Would they have time?

John could sense Mike's understanding and repentance and gave him time to process the implications but, eventually spoke again to use the teachable moment. "Our opportunity here is to show your people how serious you are about change. You see, one of the greatest signals you can send is one of humility and vulnerability. I suggest you admit your mistake and apologize not only to that team but to the whole staff as well. Explain the whole situation and how you handled it out of your old way of thinking.

But you have to change your thinking and tell them what you are going to do instead. Exhibiting humility and becoming vulnerable shows great strength and causes your people to want to join with you."

Mike was relieved and thought about sharing with John about the coffee/cappuccino machine. But, John beat him to it. "I also heard about the new coffee/cappuccino machine you bought for the employees" John said. "Given the signal you sent about the fire extinguisher what signal did you send with the purchase of the new machine?"

The conflicting signal was immediately obvious to Mike and he wondered how just a few seconds ago he was proud of that purchase. "I'm not sure", Mike stammered, "but I know it wasn't good". John prompted Mike by asking what he thought the employees felt or thought about having their request turned down because of cost, and then an expensive machine shows up.

Mike thought about that and responded that they would feel rejected or unworthy of responsibility. They would probably resent him for that.

John added that a fire extinguisher represented a value on the safety of others and a coffee machine represented an egotistical value of Mike wanting approval from the team. "So", John clarified, "You expected the outcome of better employee moral but got the unexpected results that were opposite. Do you see how easy it is to send signals when you don't use a pattern that dry tests for side effects? It's important for your core team to be part of any signal messaging activities no matter how small you think it is; especially, when you are just learning this principle. I'm going to use our previous pattern to summarize these signals:"

1. Denying the volunteers recommendation when you had asked for them to be part of the solution

   - Your <u>Words</u> were asking for their input to evaluate the company equipment.
   - Your <u>Action</u> was not acknowledging their input and denying that value.
   - The <u>Signal</u> to them is your trust is conditional based upon how you see things.

- The <u>Hope</u> is diminished for improved working conditions and pride in where they work.

2. Purchase of the coffee machine

   - Your <u>Words</u> were asking for their input and that you valued their safety.
   - Your <u>Action</u> was placing a higher value on nice things over safety.
   - The <u>Signal</u> to them is you're more concerned with how you look than them.
   - The <u>Hope</u> is diminished for improved working conditions and pride in where they work.

The three members in the room were silent, thinking about what had just transpired. Finally, Robert spoke up and suggested that the coffee machine purchase could enhance their signaling opportunity by wrapping it into the apology session described before. Why not get feedback from the group if that was something they should keep or was there something else that could better improve their environment. John nodded and said they had now tweaked their original communication and the complete process is to dry test the 'tweak' for possible side effects.

After doing that and deciding that the course of action was appropriate John switched to a new line of thinking on the same topic.

"Mike", John started, "Your actions in this instance affected more than the team that volunteered to do the research project and it's important to try to repair relationships with everyone who is directly involved. So I ask that you consider how this impacted Jana and Robert."

Mike knew that Jana had seemed bothered lately and Robert seemed to be avoiding him so, without further prompting he apologized to them right away. Robert was quick to forgive Mike's humanity and said it was a good lesson for him as well. Jana, however, was still holding back.

After glancing at John and seeing his nod to go ahead she spoke up," earlier this week I talked to you about Charlie's conversation about the direction shifts we've been making and how they could have a negative effect on the other team members. But you just blew me off and excused his behavior. I was so mad at you, not just because you dismissed me but, mostly because it seemed like you wanted to avoid a crucial conversation with Charlie. If Charlie really feels like that, then avoiding the conversation it will just allow the attitude to grow in our business. If we really believe in our new direction, then we can't avoid taking on the difficult tasks.

Both John and Mike picked up on her use of the word "our". John recognized it as a symptom of engagement; Mike felt a new enhanced respect for her commitment. Eventually, Mike found the words to recognize her keen sensitivity to the issue and apologized for his lack of the same and promised to rectify the issue. Their relationship was again made whole.

In this session Mike and the core team also reexamined the full list of recommendations from the research committee and agreed that even though there were a few questionable items, they would accept the entire list to send a signal of trust to that team. The ghost of fix it or make it do was being exorcised from Mike's thinking.

Chapter Ten

BUILDING THE DESIGNED CULTURE

In the weeks that followed Mike moved his office downstairs and even took a step further by replacing his cherry office furniture with a used metal desk and credenza. His old space was turned into a nice break room for the staff. He re-hung the portraits of the company founders in the company's reception area and hung a dartboard in the new break room.

John continued the weekly sessions and during those he taught the core team about the three components of a high functioning culture. The first week he taught about the physical component. The team was actively addressing this by improving the equipment and moving the break room to a nicer location.

3 Components of Cultural Design:

1. Physical
2. Emotional
3. Cognitive

"The physical component is described as anything that impacts a person's energy such as resources or tools to do a job; temperature, light, or noise levels; positivity or negativity from co-workers or a supervisor; job demands; or co-worker and supervisor relationships is part of the physical component[3,4,5]." John warned the team that the physical component was sometimes the easiest to deliver but unfortunately, many companies stop there, falsely thinking that they have done something impressive.

The following week John explained what was involved in the emotional component. "An individual team member who exhibits the emotional component" John exclaimed, "is described as one who is totally self-invested in one's job. This is usually called engagement. So how do you get your people "totally invested or engaged"?

Research from The Gallup Organization found that engagement begins with the person's direct supervisor since they have significant control over the job variables such as demands and resources and have authority over the worker. It is usually the supervisor who can make or break engagement[2].

We've already spent a lot of time on the principle of **Signaling**. Signaling tells the worker how much they can trust the leadership by its actions[6]. Your integrity and degree of trustworthiness is based on the gap that is observed between your words and actions; the wider the gap, the lower the probability of sustainable engagement.

Variables of Emotional Engagement:

1. Signaling
2. Shared Vision
3. Values
4. Leadership Style

"The next variable of the emotional component" John continued, "is a **Shared Vision** that becomes an impressive force of power in people's hearts. People desire to be connected to something that is important and that deeply matters to them[7]. Work becomes part of pursuing a larger purpose and uplifts people's spirits. The role of your leadership is to transform the self-interests of your team members into the collective interests of this organization's mission and vision."

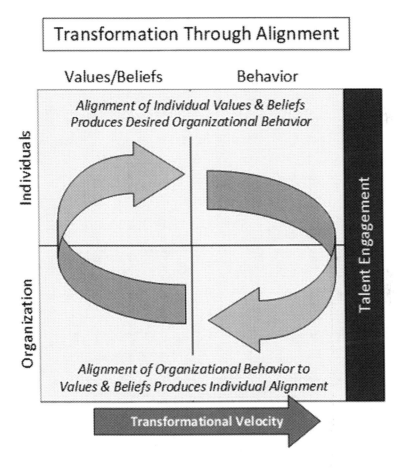

John realized that he was beginning to push the limits of his audience but felt he needed to develop the next 3 points quickly. "High performing organizations also have specific Values that are a part of the daily conversation throughout their organization[8]. When these values are aligned with personal values they become the internal drivers of outward behavior[9].

When the individual's values are much different from the values of an organization, a gap is created[10]. When the gap between personal and organizational values is small, the employee has a higher probability of sustainable engagement especially if it is combined with a higher level of trust.

The **Leadership Style** that is most likely to foster engagement is called transformational leadership. The old style like your father and grandfather used and we recently saw in Tom Barkley is called "command and control". That style will not be effective with today's younger generation.

Transformational leaders focus on followers, motivating them to high levels of performance, and in the process, developing their own leadership potential[11].

They are able to bring about feelings of passion and identification with the work. They intellectually stimulate and encourage followers to become creative and explore new ways of doing things.

They foster supportive relationships and open lines of communication so that followers feel free to share ideas and receive direct recognition for their contributions. The relationship with the follower's immediate supervisor becomes highly valued and employee retention remains high. Therefore, transformational leadership has the highest probability of obtaining sustainable engagement[12]."

The next week John was ready to deliver his final point on the three components of cultural design. Fortunately, the team still seemed ready for more so he launched in. Lastly folks, the **Cognitive component** is the individual's personal connection with the performance of the work[12]. To achieve this connection, two development activities are required: Leadership and Right Roles.

Leadership development is not limited to those who have a title; every person in your company has responsibilities and is a potential leader thus, every employee needs a development plan to take them to a higher level. Creating a climate of continual learning and growth is one of the most powerful factors found for retaining employees and building sustained engagement[7]. John noticed the puzzled look on Jana's face and added, "A development climate sends a signal to every person that the company cares for them; and that creates another emotional connection."

John continued explaining about **Leadership development**, "One of the reasons companies plateau, is described by John Maxwell in the phrase; "Law of the Lid". Basically, it says that the organization will only grow up to the capacity of those who lead it creating a "lid on the organization. Maxwell's meaning is that it is imperative that **Leadership Development** in any organization is not just developing knowledge and skills but also self-awareness and character[2]. In his opinion, to do otherwise puts limits on the organization's development.

If the leader stops transitioning to higher levels of self-awareness and learning the organization stops and then several things happen:

a) Organizational **atrophy** compounds; *those who want to grow and expand their roles but bump up against the leader must leave to grow elsewhere or stagnate.*

b) Organizational **entropy** accelerates; *people spend more time doing less productive work.*

c) Organizational **apathy** spreads; *attitudes that demonstrate lack of commitment, caring, and enthusiasm for the company or the work prevail.*

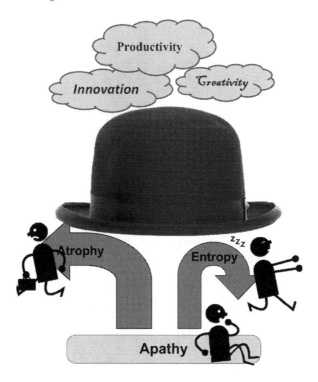

The lid restricts a company's Productivity, Innovation, and Creativity. The interesting point is that research shows that most employees desire further development and that also drives sustainable engagement[7.]. So let's consider the following:

1. Leadership development drives employee engagement.
2. Employee engagement drives customer satisfaction.
3. Customer satisfaction drives shareholder value[8.].

Leadership development must be more than learning managerial functions; it must contain full emotional development because that provides the greatest degree of leverage in attaining our full potential[7].

Cognitive development of the leader gives them self-assurance, confidence, and courage to become the transformational leader who is not fearful or egotistical about their followers succeeding beyond them.

Jana was now tracking with John and wanted to clarify what she understood. "You're saying that every person needs a development plan but the plan must be individualized to the individual. So some people may need more skills training and others may need help sharpening their natural talents, right?" "You got it" John affirmed. He then continued to teach about **Right Roles development.**

Remember, that high performing organizations develop and utilize the <u>natural talents</u> of their workforce, so it is imperative that an individual be in the **Right Role** that utilizes their natural talents a majority of the time[15]. Too many times our management education system teaches that we create a specifically detailed 'Job Description' and then we try to fit people into that role. It's a logical thing to do but much of the time it doesn't work out well.

In my opinion, it would be better to have a more general idea of the job's purpose then look for the candidate that has the most natural talent to fill that role.

It is important to get the right people on the bus, the wrong people off the bus, and the right people in the right seats[13]. The "right seats" implies that the person's natural talents along with education, skills, and experience need to fit the role the organization needs. When this is designed into the culture the outcome is more sustainable engagement inside the company.

Let me also say that a person can be engaged in one role, but not become engaged in another[14]. This means climbing the corporate ladder may not be the right career choice for an individual or a company. (Oh, and by the way, this also means the 'corporate ladder' may be an outdated concept of promotion and status.)

Therefore, the **cognitive component** points to intrinsic motivation that is over and above good working conditions or pay; it is the opportunity to do what one does best every day and the challenge to personally grow in a meaningful workplace.

Chapter Eleven

BREAKING THE CORPORATE LADDER RUNGS

Jana had not forgotten about Charlie's sabotaging talk and she had been collecting more evidence of his undercutting behavior. At John's next session she took the opportunity to discuss Charlie with Mike, Robert, and John.

Jana presented the evidence against Charlie to the group and then said, "Initially I was so mad that I wanted him to be gone—fired. Then, our talk about leadership development forced me to consider another alternative and one that we should follow until we are proven wrong. And that is that Charlie must have the opportunity to decide if he values development over termination. So, I've been watching him closely and talking to customers and team members about what they appreciate most about Charlie.

What I found out is that he has outstanding performance in the field with patients and is intuitively competent with knowledge and skills. The teams confirm that and, in high stress emergency situations they would rather have him directing operations than anyone else because he kept his cool and saw the bigger picture."

Mike spoke up and suggested that maybe he was in the wrong role as a shift supervisor and they should demote him to an ambulance EMT. Robert said that would reduce his pay and probably cause more problems than it fixed, or he would get mad and leave. John just listened as the interaction continued.

Mike didn't want to lose him if he could be turned away from the 'dark side' referencing his fondness of Star Wars. Robert started talking about Susan taking Charlie's position, but it was Jana who came up with an innovative thought and directed the discussion.

"I think our conversation is being framed by the corporate ladder concept" she said. "How can we change the corporate ladder 'rules' and create a winning solution?

How would Charlie respond if we asked him to be an EMT trainer; someone who is always in the field and rode with different teams? When there is a high stress emergency then he is designated as the situational leader for all operations. In this role, he maintains his pay and does what he seems to do best. It could actually be a promotion."

Now John spoke up, "Before you make an offer like this you need to find out if he is 'Actively Disengaged' or just on the negative side of 'Not Engaged'. So, I think you will need to discuss with him your findings, tell him that his behavior is not acceptable for anyone, much less a supervisor.

If he gets defensive and tries to justify his position, then he probably is Actively Disengaged and should be let go. Otherwise I think he could be turned around and the change in position may help him become more engaged. The next question is who should have the talk with him?"

Mike was surprised at John's question. He assumed the task would naturally fall on him which made his stomach turn and his heart beat faster. Mike did not like confrontation and preferred to avoid it when possible. "I thought I would have to do it" Mike said, "What other options are there?"

"Mike, you already have a core management team right here. Robert is now a shift supervisor, but Jana is still your assistant. I propose that Jana has already shown her leadership qualities and commitment to your organization. So why not put her in the right role and give her the title and authority that fits her talents?

The reason I'm mentioning this now is that business growth depends on developing your leaders. They are already accepted as influential leaders by the employees therefore, by having a formal recognition by you, another positive signal can be sent to the group that you are not afraid to promote or relinquish control. In effect, you lift the 'lid' a little higher."

A wave of relief flowed over Mike as he thought about sharing responsibilities. He was so excited about taking the next step that he almost forgot about having a talk with Charlie. "So, what role could we put Jana and Robert in?"

John suggested that Jana and Robert leave the room so he could have a personal discussion with Mike. When they left John turned to Mike and asked him, "What do you really want, Mike? Early on you told me that you were a teacher and were pressed into service to run this company. Do you still want to do this, or would you rather be doing something else?"

Mike's relief now turned to shock and was quickly followed by fear. "I don't know, I mean, it's not that I haven't thought about going back to teaching or somehow working with young people. But how could I do that? Who would hire me and what would happen to the business?"

John knew that he had thrown Mike a curve ball, but he also knew that Mike had an opportunity to make some life changes in the coming months after the union vote was concluded. "Over the last several weeks we've been talking about getting the right people in the right roles so they can excel and engage fully. That also includes you.

Maybe we could work things out where you can do what you want to do and are best at. My suggestion is that we work Jana into the role of company President, Robert into the role of Chief Operating Officer, and you become the Chief Executive Officer.

As CEO your job would be to work yourself out of daily operations and let Jana take over the marketing and business decisions. I'm confident that she can do a great job; she has the talent to be tough when she needs to be and yet be someone people relate to (a padded steel rod, so to speak).

You can reduce your involvement over a one year period and begin pursuing your passion again. One other thing to consider is you will probably need to give up some ownership or pay out some form of profit sharing, so your people have a stake in the results."

Mike hadn't been expecting this but, it resonated peace. So, without much handwringing he agreed that it seemed like a solution he could back. So, they called Robert and Jana back in and explained their thinking. They discussed what signal this would send and tested it for unintended consequences. By lunchtime it was decided to move forward with the change and Jana's first act after informing the group and answering questions would be to talk with Charlie.

30 days later the company had adjusted to the leadership shifts well and saw even more positive things getting done faster. Charlie had accepted the new role eagerly and his demeanor had changed as well, praising Mike and the leadership team for their efforts.

It had now been 90 days since John had first agreed to work with Mike. The company had seen numerous changes, some big, some small; but the most impacting changes came from the careful change in how the leadership communicated to the company.

The signals, as seen, heard, or felt began to change the minds of many employees. They, in turn, began to express positive observations to others or even challenge the vocal complaints of the more negative ones. The core team was seeing the results of their work and was hopeful that the union vote would go in their favor, but it was still up in the air.

They needed something more to close the deal.

Chapter Twelve

RELEASE THE HOUNDS!

With 30 days to go before the vote Mike found out through his real estate contacts that a new ambulance transport service would be opening in the metro area about the time the union vote would take place. John and the core team met to discuss the news.

"I was hoping that this wouldn't happen until the vote was over so we could focus on how to counteract their impact" Mike began. "I'm afraid we're going to lose too many hospital contracts to survive."

Robert jumped in, "Charlie, Susan, and I can work extra hard on the customer service angle with our teams and shore up any faltering relationships." But it was Jana that had the insight and confidence to speak out now,

"Gentlemen, this is the opportunity we've been looking for to firmly defeat the unionization of the company. Our people will rally together to take on this common threat. The signal we send must be informative and inspiring by identifying the threat, giving the vision of how we are going to react to it, and seeking their help to combat it. Our people will rise to the occasion and maybe recognize that a union will not be in their best long-term interests. We will, in effect, release the hounds of our entire workforce!"

John said nothing but he was thinking how his work in turning around this company was complete. People were rising up to new levels of energy, innovation, and excellence in their adjusted roles that fit their natural talents. Attitudes had shifted to a positive flow.

Soon innovation and creativity would provide new and greater opportunities. Employee and customer turnover would drop significantly, and everyone would see their paychecks increase as profits increased. He hoped they would retain him as their business coach so he could help them with the next stage of business growth.

Jana scheduled a time when both shifts could hear the news about the new competitor. It was Mike who delivered that news and then turned the floor over to Jana to give more details and inspire the 'hounds'. "…okay" Jana began, "that was the bad news of how this could negatively impact our lives, now let's look at what we can do about it and take advantage of the opportunity."

And with that, she challenged them with working hard at finding opportunities to strengthen relationships with their customers and patients. She encouraged them to take chances with leadership and be open about concerns so they could be addressed more quickly. She described how the company would look and feel like using the 'Employees Point of View' she and Mike had written up during the early days of John's coaching.

"People", she concluded, "We can not only overcome this adversary, we can come out as the number one provider in the four-state region! Are you with us?" The overwhelming response was yes. The buzz of energy in the bay stayed high that whole week. With only 29 days to go before the vote the core team was confident in the direction they were heading.

Several mornings later Mike pulled into a parking space, got out the car, and began walking to the front door. He saw Jeremy Perkins was at the door, obviously waiting for him. The union organizer seemed perturbed Mike thought; maybe because he heard about the changes they had been making. This time Mike did not want to avoid him like before. In his mind Mike wanted to say "nanny nanny boo boo" to Jeremy, but he held back.

"Mr. Post", Jeremy called out, "I need to speak with you". Mike stopped and watched the overweight weasel in the red power tie make his way toward him. "Mr. Post", began Jeremy, "I don't know what you promised them or threatened them with but it's clear that you have done something to change the feelings around here. Therefore, the union is rescinding the offer for your employees to establish a union in your company," as he handed Mike an envelope. "There will be no vote". And with that, Jeremy turned around and huffed back to his car.

The hounds were winning!

Chapter Thirteen

WHAT YOU SOW

A cheer arose up from the assembled shifts when the news that the vote had been rescinded by the union. Robert offered each shift $300 to celebrate with any way the wanted as long as it didn't impact the quality of their service.

On Susan's shift they discussed having pizza or a banquet meal together. It wasn't until a small voice spoke up and suggested they make a donation to a food bank or something, that the voices quieted, and the small voice went on to suggest, "What about a donation to the wounded veterans? We seem to transport a lot of them to and from the rehab facility." The faces on the shift looked at each other and it was decided to do that. Susan was very proud of the small voice and took her aside to tell her that. Carol's large and stout frame did not fit the small voice she had but, Carol told Susan that her personal development plan was helping her become more confident to speak out and recognize that she had value to the team.

Word of the 1st shift's donation quickly reached the other shift and they decided to donate their 'celebration money' to a similar need. Jana, Mike, and Robert decide to match the donations out of their own pockets. When John heard what was happening, he put $300 into the pool too.

Somehow a local TV station heard about the donations and interviewed Mike and Jana as a local interest story. "Our celebration turned into celebrating those who have given such a high price for our community" Mike was quoted in the story's sound bite.

In the following weeks, requests for service increased and several customers that were on the border of leaving for the competition signed fresh contracts with the 'new' old company.

John was confident that his job, for now, was finished. He met with the core team for one last session. "Let's debrief about our time together so far" John started by talking about culture.

- We know that culture is either created by evolution or it is designed.
- Culture is driven by positive and negative energy.
- A good culture requires 4 times more positive than negative charges just to remain static.
- It is easier to have a negative culture (the brain has a bias towards negativity[17]).
- It is much harder to have a positive culture that promotes growth and great success.

Trustworthiness, in an organization, is built on actions that employees hope to see. You can boil hope down into these needs: Security—in the present and future; Purpose—that their work has reason and meaning; Fulfillment—that they will have personal growth or happiness.

We meet those needs when our actions and decisions align with our words. Anything that communicates with people is called a signal. Signals may contain multiple messages and may create unintended consequences.

One of your objectives as leaders is to build trustworthiness by clearly communicating with your people keeping in mind that <u>Signaling Expresses Quality of Integrity.</u> Trustworthiness is a result of clear communications combining with aligned actions. You can already see the beginning benefits of doing that.

Therefore, you must deliberately <u>Design Your Culture</u> to maximize your leadership efforts. Your work is to have <u>Consistent Positive Signals to Build Trust</u>. Test your signals to make sure they are aligned with your design and <u>Anticipate Unintended Consequences</u>.

Commit to continuously improve who you are and what you know. BE a better person by continuous self-development then follow-through with what you DO, and you will HAVE great abundance.

I expect great things from this company if you keep up the path you are on now. In fact, research shows that companies that meet their employee hopes and design a culture that allows people to flourish through engagement will generate 2.5 times more shareholder wealth than other similar companies[15].

There is actually a lot of research that has been done that proves that employee engagement is the only sustainable competitive advantage a company has, which produces substantially more than companies using the old-style motivation techniques[18,19].

I am really impressed with the donations that were made by your people and that the idea originated by a small voice in the pack of your employees. It indicates that your journey as a company is just beginning and that the seeds have been sown which will produce good fruit if you keep the weeds out." John paused and then suggested that they move on to what is next.

THE END IS REALLY THE BEGINNING

"What I want to do now is show you a model of how to mature as a company. I won't go into depth at this time but just introduce the path". John handed each of them a page with the following diagram:

Transformational Maturity Model

John began teaching, "The 7 Layer Transformational Maturity Model illustrates how companies and individuals mature and where they get stuck: Maturity typically happens by moving accumulatively from one layer to the next following Maslov's theory of Hierarchy. Accumulatively means we always maintain our connection to the previous layers and can flow back and forth between them. Here are 3 rules that govern moving between layers:

Three rules governing movement between layers:

1. Businesses & People filter perceptions through the level they are on.
2. Businesses & People's behavior is only <u>sustainable</u> at the level they are truly on.
3. Businesses & People move to the next level as they become secure; yet, <u>strive for more</u>.

The most resilient and profitable corporations master and operate from all seven levels. The model is really about people and how they grow within the company. In fact, <u>the model is virtually the same for individuals</u> as it is for a company. Today, we will just focus on the company and how it can become great.

In **Layer 1**, a business must survive to pursue profit, shareholder value, and purpose. This layer has several goals: it must go through the processes of start-up; producing its product and getting it out to people who will buy it; and most significant is to reach positive cash flow and set aside enough cash to cover emergency relief. This is the stage where most small businesses fail. It takes a lot of effort to move the heavy flywheel of organizational momentum.

While it is probably the hardest to start a company and survive, even companies with age can face times when survival is at stake such as your 75-year-old company. So, what we have been doing is dropping back to shore up the survival level.

You're a good example of what many companies go through. Early on they have success and they keep pressing forward to grow and add to their success. But, a common problem with growth is they have not secured the foundation of the layer they are passing through or, over time, they have left an emphasis on keeping those principles alive and strong.

Layer 2 is about relationships. We have been revamping your relationships by working with your people, your customers, vendors, and even between you as a leadership team. Without relationships an organization does not truly exist. This layer requires reasonably stable critical relationships to provide the means to grow while surviving.

Layer 3 is about competence. There is a sense of organizational accomplishment and achievement and survival is no longer the main issue. The daily maintenance of operations becomes consuming while improving the systems and processes becomes the struggle. The company remains inwardly focused.

This is also the layer that is the most seductive to the leaders of the company. They may feel they are at the top of their game and the company is ready to expand.

Successful leaders can develop excessive self-assurance, arrogance, or ambition and can make unwise choices in the means of growth, leading to a company's downfall or irrelevance. Or, similar to what happened here, success and profitability produce complacency and the company spends its resources maintaining good enough, which can make them vulnerable to market shifts and disruptive technologies.

However, good leadership that is committed to becoming a great company will seriously pursue **Layer 4** of transformation. The focus shifts to becoming a learning organization with people development at the top of the list.

Leadership thinking patterns change from operational issues to developing other leaders and the culture. A critical factor is getting the right people on board and in the right positions. Management must shift their leadership style to allow room for newer leaders to grow and develop. This is the time to search out and break old thinking patterns. Leaders should become inspirational; breathing new life into the organization.

| **The Law of the Transformation—** | An organization can transform only to the degree the leadership's actions align with their words. |

a. Change is not transformation. Change is like a course correction for a boat; Transformation is the boat taking on the ability to fly.

b. Organizational Transformation is a parallel shift of consciousness between individuals and the organization itself. (see quadrant below.)

c. Alignment combined with engagement creates the velocity needed to achieve Organizational Transformation.

Let's revisit the Transformation Through Alignment quadrant again. There are three components that propel the organization towards transformation:

1. An individual's values and beliefs align with the organizational values and beliefs.

2. Individuals see the organization practicing and behaving in alignment with those written values and beliefs.

3. Leadership promotes an environment for engagement to occur.

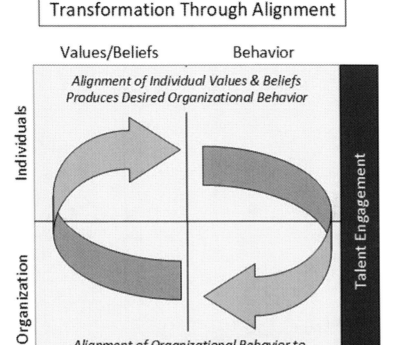

Transformation Through Alignment

When the organization has a critical mass of its people aligned and engaged the organization will undergo transformation. The process is additive and creates the velocity needed for transformation or moving to the next level of growth.

Leadership is the key to producing alignment by first defining their values, mission, and vision and then living them. Living the values, mission, and vision involves consistently valuing the stories that demonstrate behaviors needed to comply. Of course, it is most important that the leaders are the first ones to set the examples.

Leadership is also the key to producing engagement by encouraging personal and leadership development. They must live a management style that encourages participation and feedback, and recognition for engaged behavior. If those who are not aligned do not exit on their own then, leadership should help them get off the bus.

The results of the previous layer begin to show in **Layer 5**. The organization increasingly demonstrates a balance between culture, leadership, and operations. Company values and vision are clear to all and there is a disciplined culture of execution. The successes of the past could lead to hubris in leadership, but now is the time for humility blended with strength.

Engaged employees are those who find themselves consistently doing what they do best. Trust is built through experience. They trust their leaders and believe in the value of what they are doing. Innovation, creativity, higher productivity, lower operating costs, and higher revenues are the outcomes of this layer.

In **Layer 6** the organization has impact and uses its position to influence the industry it represents, the marketplace where its reputation is built, and the lives of the people who work for it and their customers. It makes a positive difference in the world.

Layer 7 represents a service level that permeates the company. The heart of the organization has grown enough to embrace its responsibility as a community member. It is also in the heart of the organization's individual members. It goes beyond finding activities that "make good PR" or are revenue motivated and seeks philanthropic outlets to share their success.

The 7 Layer model is not always a linear progression. It's more like puzzle pieces. If one of the pieces disconnects, you must go back to the previous layer and reconnect it. Sometimes the business will jump ahead and dabble in an advanced layer but, eventually the stresses at that level will reveal a poor foundation at the previous level and they will always fall back to the layer they are truly on. (Remember the 3 Rules governing movement between layers.)

The most resilient and profitable corporations master and operate from all seven levels. The model is really about people and how they grow within the company. In fact, the model is virtually the same for individuals as it is for a company.

The Success Formula relates to the balance of goals needed at each level. All 7 layers need a strong 'DO' or operational discipline but, in the early stages of organizational maturity, Layers 1-3 'DO' will have more emphasis.

All 7 layers need a good 'BE' or cultural discipline but, as the organization matures, Level 5-7 'BE' beginning to have more emphasis.

Finally, all 7 layers need strong '+' or leadership and its emphasis must be to provide the right balance and continuously be improving and developing their capabilities and the consciousness layers of their people."

John knew he was on his soapbox of passion, but he couldn't stop now. "The difference between good and great can be a very small amount of hard work that produces a disproportionate amount of results. When you get down to the root cause of

> **"Good companies are great at what they do.
> Great companies are good at who they are."**

the difference between GOOD companies and GREAT ones you'll find that GREAT companies are better at balancing the three core priorities of: DOing, Leadership, and BEing.

The question is, "what resources are available to your organization that has the capacity to adapt, innovate, strive, achieve, or create? Resources like this will create a Sustainable Competitive Advantage. Therefore, it should have the highest value to you. The only resources with those qualities are your own people.

Many companies use the phrase, "People are our greatest asset." But they don't really believe it because the phrase is not really true. The true saying would be more like this: *The right people, when aligned and engaged, are our greatest asset.* When the right people are aligned around common values, vision, and mission AND they are emotionally engaged they invariably produce a Sustainable Competitive Advantage.

It has been my honor to serve you these last several months and it has been rewarding and fun to work with you. I hope that you will continue to use me as your coach in the future.

And on that note, Jana and Mike insisted that they all go out for a great dinner on the company dime.

CAN OUR BOAT LEARN TO FLY?

A year has gone by and the ambulance company was now at the "Competence" level of maturity. Income had increased because the increased emphasis on service had strengthened the relationships with service providers which, in turn, reduced contract turnover. This also reduced the costs for sales to find new customers to replace the ones who had dropped their services.

Employee turnover had dropped due to better working conditions and increasing trust in the management team. With Jana and Robert taking the lead, all processes and policies were reevaluated to either streamline for effectiveness or discard entirely. The business was running smoothly.

Things were going so well that Mike was beginning to make plans for his eventual exit. Jana was building a network of business contacts. She even had an inquiry for a position with the competition. Roger, however, was uneasy with the competence level they had achieved. He dug through his notes to the last day when John (the coach) had summarized the vision for building a great company.

John had talked about how success can seduce the leaders of the company into complacency or making unwise decisions. He had said that going from Level 3 Competence to Level 4 Transformation is very difficult and many companies fail to make it. Roger decided to put this topic on the agenda for the next management huddle. In the meantime, he suggested to Jana that they invite John to come back and sit in at that meeting which she did.

John was happy to come back and hear how things were going. Like usual, Jana recited the performance metrics for company before turning the meeting over to Roger.

Roger started out summarizing about the changes the company had made and how the environment in the service bays and attitudes of the employees had improved. Then he quoted from John's notes:

"Change is not transformation. Change is like a course correction for a boat; Transformation is the boat taking on the ability to fly."

If we want a sustainable competitive advantage then, what are we doing to reach escape velocity and transform ourselves into a great company? What growth opportunities do we have for our employees? What opportunities are we missing because we spend our time steering the boat instead of making it fly?

The room fell silent as each reflected on Roger's declaration. Jana's sharp mind and self-awareness quickly picked up on what Roger was getting at. She thought about her own recent thoughts about the competitor's position inquiry and how her ego was beginning to inflate.

Mike's hopes of a quick exit diminished as he thought about his legacy falling back into its previous state. John was thrilled that they had come to this place and his coaching was validated by the longevity of his efforts not being lost.

Jana spoke first, "Thank you Roger for bringing our vision back into focus. John, I believe you had taught us that transformation requires escape velocity through people development. And the first people to develop was us. Is that correct?"

"Yes Jana, that's correct", John began, "It is usually very hard for a management team shift their primary focus from operations, where they are having the satisfaction of seeing progress made, to the cultural development of employees and new leaders.

"You have done well getting the wrong people off the bus and generally, you have the right people on the bus. The mind shift is difficult but, imperative: <u>get the right people in the right seats</u>. That raises the question of fitting a person into a specific role or fitting the role for a specific person.

Historically, job descriptions specify the details and requirements and, a person is chosen by their experience, education, and temperament to fill the role. Using this pattern generally produces mixed results but not the results that are great.

While there is not a right or wrong way to create a job position and fill it, I do believe there is an option to the historical pattern. The option is to understand how a person's behavior is naturally hard-wired. Then modify the job description to fit that natural hard wiring. It may mean some creative restructuring of roles.

When you fit a person to fill the job description, they will modify their behavior to adapt to what is needed. However, under stressful conditions the modification is overshadowed when the person reverts to their "natural" state. Adapting behavior, at best, produces "good" performance. A person who operates in their natural state can produce "great" performance.

The tool we use to identify the hard wiring is the CliftonStrengths 34° assessment by the Gallup Organization. It has, by far, the best granularity for usefulness in an organization.

Each strength has its own description of what it naturally looks like and how it operates in real life. Using this tool, we can create teams by strengths profiles and then identify the people who best fit the profiles found on each team."

John continued, "consider how a football team executes a play. Every player has a role based upon what they do best. The quarterback analyzes the situation and selects the play to execute. The linemen need to understand the defense, who to block, and which direction to block. The backs and ends know the route to run for a pass or who to block. When the ball is snapped everyone works using their strengths to move the ball downfield. I call this choreography. Team members need to understand how to hand off work when it leaves their strength area and is a better fit for another team member.

I'm handing you a sheet with some sample role profiles. A profile contains key strengths that are critical for achieving great results. Once you understand how each of the strengths operates and what it looks like in operation, you'll realize why it is more fluid than a job description."

Sample Role Profiles for XYZ Company

Role	Desired Strength	Leadership Theme
	Connectedness	Thinking
	Futuristic	Thinking
CEO	Ideation	Thinking
	Positivity	Influencing
	Strategic	Thinking
	Communication	Relating
	Activator	Executing
Company President	Analytical	Thinking
	Command	Influencing
	Competition	Influencing
	Self-Assurance	Executing
	Achiever	Executing
	Arranger	Thinking
Admin Assistant	Communication	Relating
	Consistency	Thinking
	Responsibility	Relating

To maximize the effectiveness of people your best effort is to help them understand themselves and utilize what is naturally available to you.

I strongly suggest that you utilize a certified StregthsFinder coach to help train your people in the use of Strengths and incorporate it into your cultural DNA."

With that, Jana knew the next steps and, what she would implement to reach the escape velocity towards the next level. The excitement of the future had already pushed the competition's inquiry out of her mind.

Mike was comfortable feeling that the company was in good hands and he could continue to plan his exit.

References

[1] Coffman, Curt & Gonzalez-Molina, Gabriel (2002). *Follow this path: How the world's greatest organizations drive growth by unleashing human potential* New York, NY Warner Books, Inc.

[2] Maxwell, John C. (1998). *The 21 Irrefutable Laws of Leadership.* Thomas Nelson Publishers, August 1998

[3] Harter, James K., Schmidt, Frank L., Hayes, Theodore L. (2002). Business-Unit-Level Relationship Between Employee Satisfaction, Employee Engagement, and Business Outcomes: A Meta-Analysis. *Journal of Applied Psychology.* Vol. 87, No. 2, 268–279

[4] Babcock-Roberson, Meredith E. & Strickland, Oriel J. (2010). The relationship between charismatic leadership, work engagement, and organizational citizenship behaviors. *The Journal of Psychology,* 2010. 144(3), 313-326.

[5] Dollard, Maureen F.; Bakker, Arnold B. (2010). Psychosocial safety climate as a precursor to conducive work environments, psychological health problems, and employee engagement. *Journal of Occupational and Organizational Psychology* (2010), 83, 579–599.

[6] Six, Frédérique; Sorge, Arndt (2008). Creating a High-Trust Organization: An Exploration into Organizational Policies that Stimulate Interpersonal Trust Building. *Journal of Management Studies.* 45:5 July 2008

[7] Senge, Peter M. (1993). *Fifth Discipline: The Art and Practice of the Learning Organization.* New York, N.: Doubleday/Currency

[8.]Barrett, Richard (2006). *Building a Values-Driven Organization- A whole system approach to cultural transformation.* Butterworth-Heinemann, Burlington, MA. 2006

[9.]Urbany, Joel; Reynolds, Thomas; & Phillips, Joan (2008). *How to Make Values Count in Everyday Decisions.* MIT Sloan Management Review. Cambridge, MA. Summer 2008 Vol. 49 No. 4

[10.]Robbins, Stephen P., Judge, Timothy A. (2007).Organizational Behavior.—12th ed. *Pearson, Prentice Hall.*

[11.]Riggio, Ronald E. (2009). Are You a Transformational Leader? *Psychology Today @ Cutting-Edge Leadership.* Retrieved from: http://www.psychologytoday.com/blog/cutting-edge-leadership/200903/are-you-transformational-leader

[12.]Christian, Michael S., Garza, Adela S., & Slaughter, Jerel E. (2011). Work engagement: a quantitative review and test of its relations with task and contextual performance. *Personnel Psychology. 64,* 89–136

[13.]Collins, James C. (2001). *Good to Great; why some companies make the leap and others don't.* HarperCollins Publishers Inc. New York, NY

[14.]Kahn, W. A. (1990). Psychological conditions of personal engagement and disengagement at work. *Academy of Management Journal,* 33, 692–724.

[15.]Fleming, John H., Asplund, Jim (2007). *Human Sigma; managing the employee customer encounter.* New York, NY. Gallup Press.

[16.]Baumeister, Roy F., Bratslavsky, Ellen, Finkenauer Catrin, Vohs, Kathleen D. (2001). Bad Is Stronger Than Good. *Review of General Psychology.* 2001, Vol. 5. No. 4. 323-370

[17.]Peeters, G., & Czapinski, J. (1990). Positive-negative asymmetry in evaluations: The distinction between affective and informational negativity effects. In W. Stroebe & M. Hewstone (Eds.), *European review of social psychology* (Vol. 1, pp. 33-60). New York: Wiley.

18. Senge, Peter M., Smith, Bryon; Kruschwitz, Nina; Laur, Joe; Schley, Sara. (2010). The Necessary Revolution: Working together to create a sustainable world. New York, NY. Broadway Books, an imprint of The Crown Publishing Group a division of Random House, Inc.

19. Asplund, Jim, Fleming, John H. Ph.D., & Harter, James Ph.D. (2007). *Return on Investment in Engaging Employees.* Gallup Management Journal. Retrieved from: http://gmj. gallup.com/content/102523/Return-Investment-Engaging-Employees.aspx